# My
# CIVIL WAR
## Ancestor

# A Zap The Grandma Gap Activity Book

# By Janet Hovorka & Amy Slade

# How To Use This Book

This activity book is designed to help create stronger bonds in modern families by encouraging the whole family to learn about their ancestors together. Greater knowledge about family history especially strengthens and empowers youth by creating self-esteem, resilience and a greater sense of control over their lives. Studying the family's past also strengthens the relationships between living family members by creating a shared experience and core identity that no one else in the world can duplicate. Young people can take the lead to accomplish the activities in this book with their family members.

It is our hope that learning about your family's past together can be a fun and exciting adventure and that this book will help all of your family members discover joy in the quest to find out more about your ancestors .

*Janet Hovorka*      *Amy Slade*

Copyright © 2013 by Janet Hovorka and Amy Slade
All rights reserved. No part of this publication may be distributed in any printed or electronic form without written permission.

Illustrated by Bob Bonham  http://www.coroflot.com/bbonham

While the authors have made every effort to provide accurate internet addresses at the time of publication, neither the authors nor the publisher assume any responsibility for changes that occur after publication. Further, neither the author nor publisher assume any responsibility for third party websites or their contents.

Published by Family ChartMasters
P.O. Box 1080 Pleasant Grove, Utah 84062
www.familychartmasters.com  801-872-4278
For more information, free downloads, quantity discounts and new resources go to
www.zapthegrandmagap.com

International Standard Book Number: 978-09888548-3-3

# Table of Contents

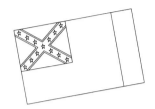 # Introduction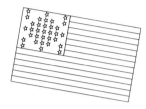

The American Civil War (also known as the War Between the States) divided the United States from 1861 to 1865. It began when several Southern states decided to form their own country apart from the rest of the United States. The states that remained were called the "Union" states or the "North" while the Southern States were called the "Confederate States of America" or the "South." The greatest issue of the war was slavery and whether or not the western territories would join the United States in support of slavery like the South, or against slavery like the North. Abraham Lincoln, the president of the Union States outlawed slavery during the war, and when the Union won the war, slavery became illegal throughout the restored United States.

Studying the lives of our Civil War Ancestors can be hard. These were extreme times in our history and many people created and suffered experiences that are hard for us to understand today. However, there are many lessons to learn from this time in our past and it is better to face that history and let it give us knowledge to improve the present. Hopefully this book will spark good discussions in your family and will help you consciously create a better future for the generations to come.

You may have several Civil War ancestors. For this book, you may want to focus on the one you know the most about, but feel free to add other pages at the end with more information about other Civil War ancestors.

## Sections of this Book

The workbook starts with pages to fill in what you know about your ancestors and instructions on where to look for more information. Then there are pages with common cultural experiences which work like puzzle pieces to help fill in what the day to day lives of your ancestors were like. The pages with references that are not specific to your family members are marked at the bottom of the page with puzzle pieces. While your ancestors may be Union or Confederate, free African Americans or slaves, you might not be sure that your ancestors experienced the details of this cultural knowledge, but these are common experiences during the Civil War and likely applicable to your family.

# How Am I Related To My Civil War Ancestors?

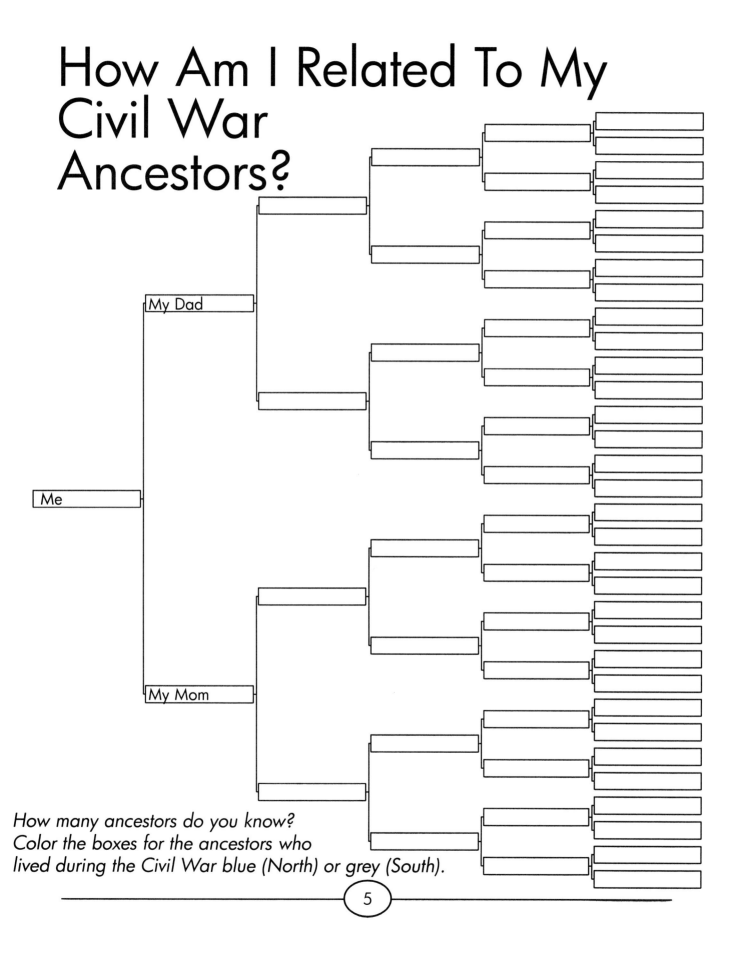

My Dad

Me

My Mom

How many ancestors do you know?
Color the boxes for the ancestors who
lived during the Civil War blue (North) or grey (South).

# Where Can I Find Information?

Look for clues about your family history around your home.

Where does your family keep their family history pictures and documents?

_____

_____

Who do you need to ask to see them?

_____

_____

Which family members can you ask about your Civil War ancestors?

_____

You could ask them:

- ☐ What do you know about our Civil War ancestors?
- ☐ How am I related to them?
- ☐ Do you know what they looked like?  Do you have any pictures?
- ☐ Do you know what their personalities were like?
- ☐ Do you have any family history keepsakes or documents?  Who does?
- ☐ Where did they live during the time of the Civil War?
- ☐ What are some stories about my Civil War ancestors?
- ☐ Do you know where our Civil War ancestors served in the military?
- ☐ Are there any recipes, talents, traditions or common sayings that come from our Civil War family history?

*Check the questions you want to ask, then arrange a time to ask the questions in a family history interview.*

# My Ancestor's Childhood

Civil War Ancestor's name _____

He/She was born on _____(date)
in_____(place)

His/Her parents were:

Mother's Name_____  Father's Name_____
Born _____(date)  Born _____(date)
_____(place)  _____(place)
Died _____(date)  Died _____(date)
_____(place)  _____(place)

His/her parents were married _____(date)
_____(place)

His/Her brothers and sisters were:

_____  _____

_____  _____

_____  _____

*Place a star next to any Civil War soldiers and put the age of each person in the year 1861 next to their name.*

# Where Can I Find Even More?

Don't fret if you don't know everything yet. Just keep looking and learning.

**nps.gov/civilwar/soldiers-and-sailors-database.htm**
The best starting place

**civilwarroster.com**
Almost all regimental rosters

**familysearch.org**
Index to Compiled Military Service Records

**fold3.com/civilwar**
Images of Compiled Military Service Records

**cyndislist.com/us/civil-war**
Links to Civil War sites

**archives.gov/forms/pdf/natf-86-pdf**
Get copies of Compiled Military Service Records

**archives.gov/forms/pdf/natf-85.pdf**
Get copies of Pension Records

**ancestry.com**
Numerous Civil War databases

**genealogybank.com**
Civil War newspapers and more

**civilwardata.com**
American Civil War Research Database

Also check the state archives for your ancestor's home

# My Ancestor's Adult Life

Civil War Ancestor's Spouse's name _____

He/She was born on _____(date)
in_____(place)

They were married _____(date)
_____(place)

These ancestors are my  *(circle the right number of "greats")*
great great great great great great great great great great grandparents.

Their children were:

_____          _____

_____          _____

_____          _____

_____          _____

_____          _____

They lived:

_____          _____

_____          _____

*Place a star next to any Civil War soldiers and put the age of each person in the year 1861 next to their name.*

# Me and My Ancestor

You are an important descendant of your Civil War Ancestor.

*Glue or draw a picture of yourself here.*

Your Name_____

Some of your special qualities are:

_____
_____
_____
_____

You inherited some of your characteristics from your ancestors.

*Draw or glue a copy of a picture of your ancestor here.*

Your Ancestor's Name_____

Some qualities that your share in common:

_____
_____
_____
_____

# Which Side?

Some families had members who fought on the Confederate (Southern) side of the war. And some families had members who fought on the Union (Northern) side of the war. And some families had members who fought on both sides of the war. Usually people were loyal to the state they lived in or where they were born.

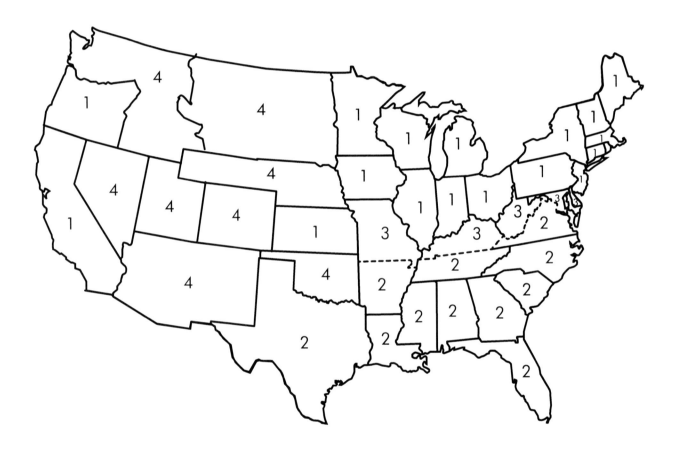

*Mark a red star where your ancestors lived.*
*1. Color all the #1 or Northern areas blue*
*2. Color all of the #2 or Southern areas red*
*3. Color all of the #3 or the border states purple*
*4. Color all of the #4 or the territories green.*

# A Tale Of Two Brothers

*Many families were divided by the Civil War. This is one true story of two brothers who were soldiers in the war.*

James and Alexander Campbell were brothers born in Scotland. In the 1850s, they both immigrated to the United States. James settled in Charleston, South Carolina and Alexander in New York.

James worked as a drayman, or cart driver, and a clerk. Before the war, he also joined a militia company called the Union Light Infantry, or the 42nd Highlanders—nicknamed for the many Scottish members of the group. Alexander also spent some time in Charleston working as a stone mason but then settled in New York. In March 1862, James's company was joined to the Confederate Army in the Charleston Battalion while up North, Alexander joined the 79th Highlander Union regiment in New York. The brothers wrote letters to each other throughout the war and years after.

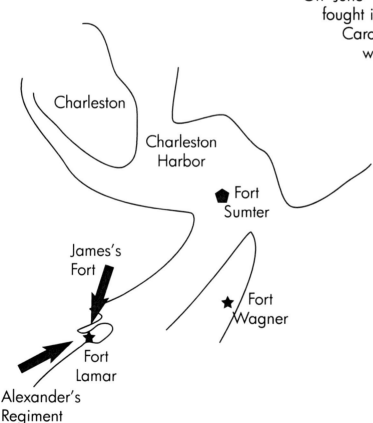

On June 16, 1862 the Campbell brothers fought in the Battle of Secessionville, South Carolina. Alex and the Union troops were attempting to capture Charleston, South Carolina by land. The Union soldiers began by attacking Fort Lamar in Secessionville. Alexander was a Color Sergeant, in charge of planting the United States flag and keeping it in place until any order to withdraw. James was a Lieutenant and fought the Union army from the fort. They fought within yards of each other but not knowing the other one was there. The Union retreated; the battle was unsuccessful for them. The Confederacy had successfully defended their capital city of Charleston from land attack.

# A Tale of Two Brothers Continued..

It wasn't until after the battle that the Campbell brothers each learned that they had directly fought each other. James wrote to Alexander, "I was astonished to hear from the prisoners that you was color Bearer of the Regmt that assaulted the Battery at this point the other day." James continued, "I was in the Brest work during the whole engagement doing my Best to Beat you(.) but I hope you and I will never again meet face to face bitter enemies on the Battlefield(.) but if such should be the case You have but to discharge your duty for your cause for I can assure you I will strive to discharge my duty to my country and my cause." James's letter was carried across the battlefield under a flag of truce. Later James attempted to visit his brother by going to Union lines and asking to see him. The officer in charge who talked to James would not let the reunion happen.

The brothers continued to exchange letters. Alexander also wrote to his wife describing how they had fought one another at Secessionville. He wrote, "it is rather bad to think that we should be fighting him on the one side and me on the other for he says he was in the fort during the whole engagement(.) I hope to god that he and I will get safe through it all and he will have his story to tell about his side and I will have my story to tell about my side."

After this particular battle James and Alexander continued to fight for their sides. Alexander was wounded in the aftermath of the second Battle of Bull Run fought August 28-30, 1862. He never fully recovered from his wound and resigned, leaving the Federal army in May 1863. James fought for the Confederacy until taken prisoner on July 18, 1863. He remained a prisoner until freed on June 12, 1865 when he returned to Charleston.

After the war, James managed a plantation and bought land south of Charleston. Alexander lived in Connecticut building a business making artistic monuments. They corresponded and were friends after the war. James died in 1907 and Alexander died in 1909.

For more information:
Johnston, Terry A. editor. *Him on the One Side and Me on the Other: The Civil War Letters of Alexander Campbell, 79th New York Infantry Regiment, and James Campbell, 1st South Carolina Battalion.* The University of South Carolina Press, Columbia, SC 2008

Power, J. Tracey. "Brother Against Brother: Alexander and James Campbells's Civil War," South Carolina Historical Magazine, 95:2 (April 1994)

# Food Rations

Hardtack was a staple food for soldiers during the Civil War. It is easy to transport and doesn't go bad. Some of the hardtack given to soldiers during the Civil War had been kept since the 1846-1848 Mexican-American War. The soldiers would put it in their coffee or hot water to soften it and drown the insects that had infested the old hardtack. Then the soldiers could skim off the insects that floated to the top and eat.

## Hardtack Recipes

### Hardtack

2 cups four
3/4 cup water
3/4 teaspoon salt
1 tablespoon shortening

Mix all ingredients thoroughly and press into a cookie sheet. Thickness should be about 1/2 inch. Sprinkle with salt if desired. Bake at 400 degrees for 30 minutes. Remove from oven and cut into squares and make holes in each cracker with a fork. Turn crackers over and bake 30 minutes on the other side. Store in an airtight container and hardtack will stay fresh as long as it is dry.

### Skillygallee

Hardtack
Hot Water
Bacon
Bacon Grease

Break the hardtack into pieces and soak in hot water until soft--about 10 minutes. While the hardtack is soaking, place the bacon in a frying pan. Remove bacon when cooked and retain bacon grease in the pan. Drain hardtack and add to the frying pan in the grease. Fry hardtack until crispy.

# Life in a War

*Using coins or buttons for place markers and dice, see if you can get through some of the common experiences that soldiers had and make it home safely to your family.*

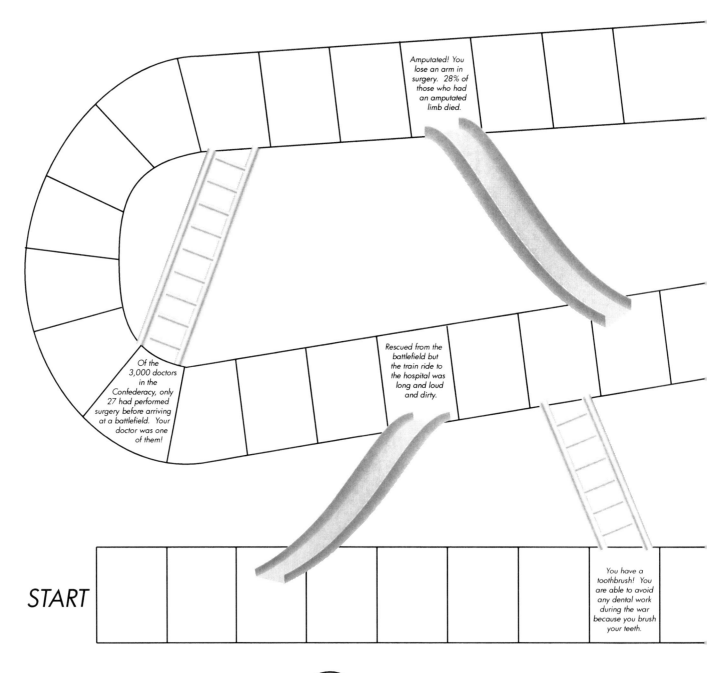

Amputated! You lose an arm in surgery. 28% of those who had an amputated limb died.

Of the 3,000 doctors in the Confederacy, only 27 had performed surgery before arriving at a battlefield. Your doctor was one of them!

Rescued from the battlefield but the train ride to the hospital was long and loud and dirty.

You have a toothbrush! You are able to avoid any dental work during the war because you brush your teeth.

START

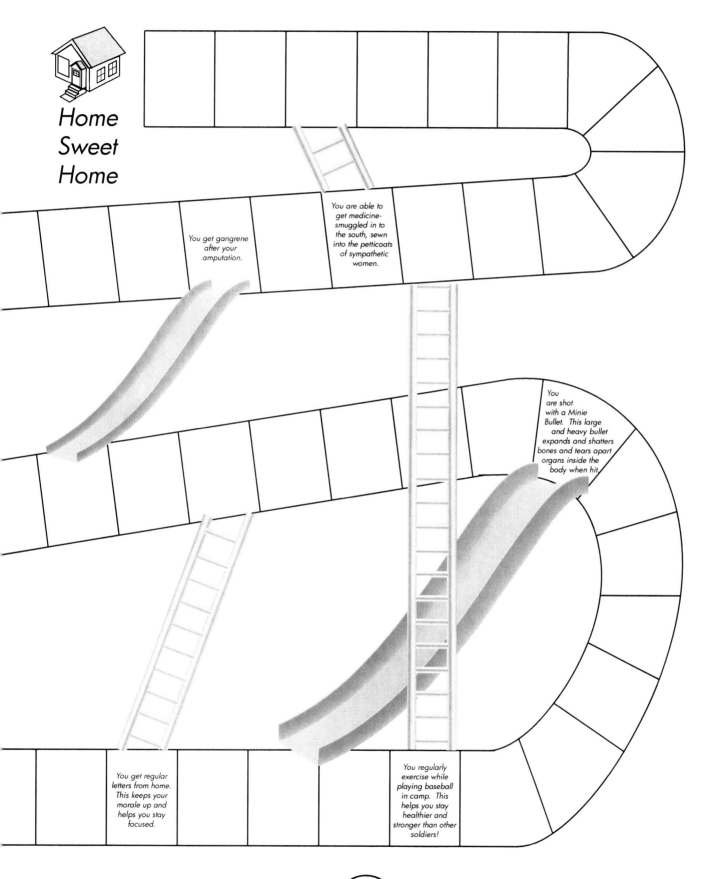

Home Sweet Home

You get gangrene after your amputation.

You are able to get medicine-smuggled in to the south, sewn into the petticoats of sympathetic women.

You are shot with a Minie Bullet. This large and heavy bullet expands and shatters bones and tears apart organs inside the body when hit.

You get regular letters from home. This keeps your morale up and helps you stay focused.

You regularly exercise while playing baseball in camp. This helps you stay healthier and stronger than other soldiers!

# Battles

These are some of the major battles in the American Civil War. Battlefields were often given two names. The Confederates often named battles for nearby towns, the Union often named them for geographic landmarks.

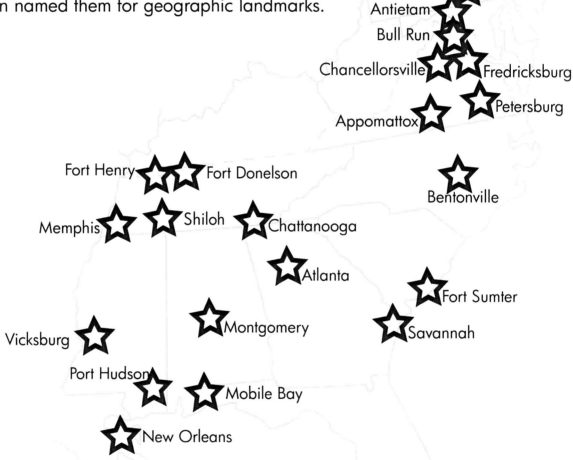

Gettysburg

Antietam

Bull Run

Chancellorsville    Fredricksburg

Appomattox    Petersburg

Bentonville

Fort Henry    Fort Donelson

Memphis    Shiloh    Chattanooga

Atlanta

Fort Sumter

Montgomery    Savannah

Vicksburg

Port Hudson

Mobile Bay

New Orleans

Color the star where your ancestor fought.
Or add a star for other battles not listed.

# My Ancestor's Timeline

*For each year enter the age of your ancestor in the box.*

☐ 1820 The Missouri Compromise keeps the balance between slave states and free states.

☐ 1850 Congress tries to compromise over the slave status of the western territories.

☐ 1860 Lincoln is elected president and one month after the election the first of eleven states secedes from the Union.

☐ 1861 The Confederate States of America is formed and Fort Sumter is attacked on April 12th. The Confederacy is victorious in the First Battle of Bull Run (Manassas).

☐ 1862 The Union defeats the Confederacy in Fort Henry, Fort Donelson, the Battle of Shiloh and the Battle of Antietam. The Confederacy is victorious at the Second Battle of Bull Run and the Battle of Fredericksburg.

☐ 1863 Lincoln issues the Emancipation Proclamation. The Confederacy has victories at Chancellorsville and Chickamauga. The Union wins the Battle of Gettysburg.

☐ 1864 The Union takes Atlanta and Savannah Georgia. Lincoln is reelected.

☐ 1865 The Union Army takes Charleston, Petersburg, and Richmond. Lee surrenders at Appomattox leading to the end of the Civil War. Lincoln is assassinated.

☐ 1870 Reconstruction continues. The 15th constitutional amendment gives the right to vote to all citizens regardless of race.

# Abraham Lincoln

Across
2. Lincoln issued the _____ Proclamation
4. _____by John Wilkes Booth
5. State Lincoln moved to when 21.
8. Lincoln's Vice President
9. State where Lincoln was born
10. Memorialized on the US coin
11. Lincoln's nickname
12. State of Lincoln's childhood home
13. Lincoln's profession before presidency

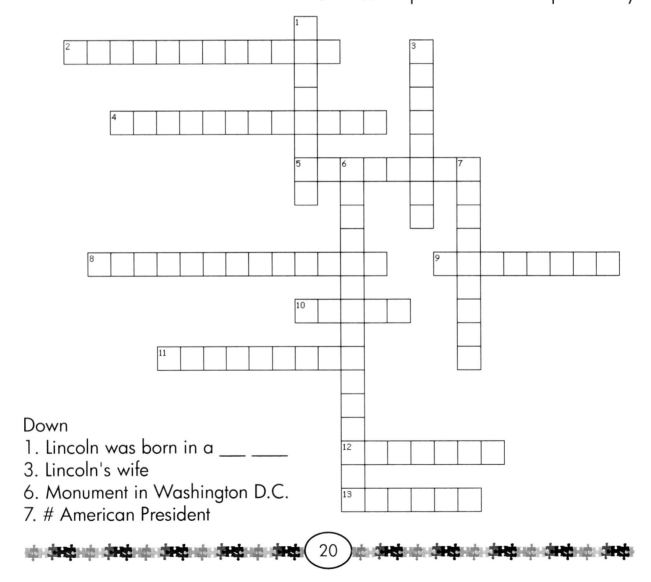

Down
1. Lincoln was born in a ___ ___
3. Lincoln's wife
6. Monument in Washington D.C.
7. # American President

# Gettysburg Address

Lincoln's dedication of the cemetery at Gettysburg is considered one of the greatest speeches in U.S. History. Few remember the first speech by another person on the program which lasted for two hours, but Lincoln's short speech is still memorized by many today. *Rearrange the fallen letters of vertical columns to discover the first part of the speech.*

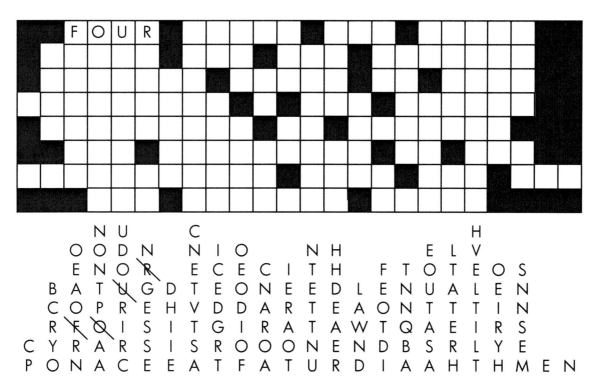

Now we are engaged in a great civil war, testing whether that nation, or any nation so conceived and so dedicated, can long endure. We are met on a great battlefield of that war. We have come to dedicate a portion of that field, as a final resting place for those who here gave their lives that that nation might live. It is altogether fitting and proper that we should do this.

But, in a larger sense, we can not dedicate, we can not consecrate, we can not hallow this ground. The brave men, living and dead, who struggled here, have consecrated it, far above our poor power to add or detract. The world will little note, nor long remember what we say here, but it can never forget what they did here. It is for us the living, rather, to be dedicated here to the unfinished work which they who fought here have thus far so nobly advanced. It is rather for us to be here dedicated to the great task remaining before us—that from these honored dead we take increased devotion to that cause for which they gave the last full measure of devotion—that we here highly resolve that these dead shall not have died in vain—that this nation, under God, shall have a new birth of freedom—and that government of the people, by the people, for the people, shall not perish from the earth.

# Color the Flags

The Confederate army changed flags several times during the war. The first flag was very similar to the Union flag and caused confusion about who was fighting whom. The second flag was this "Stainless" flag but all of the white on the flag was thought to look too much like a plain white surrender flag. Thus a large red stripe was added to the right side of the flag. Sometimes the top left section of the flag with red and the blue diagonal cross without the rest of the white section was used during army battles but it was never the official flag of the Confederacy.

*1. Color all the #1 areas red*
*2. Color all of the #2 areas blue*

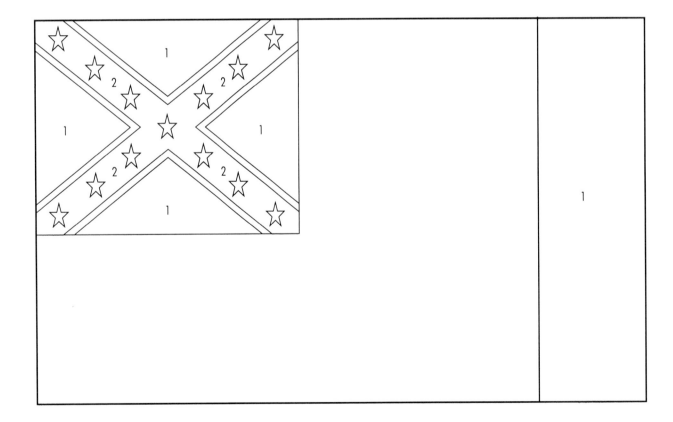

1. Color all the #1 areas red
2. Color all of the #2 areas blue

| | 1 |
|---|---|
| ☆ 2 ☆ 2 ☆ ☆ ☆ ☆ ☆ ☆ ☆ ☆ ☆ ☆ ☆ ☆ ☆ ☆ ☆ ☆ ☆ ☆ ☆ ☆ ☆ ☆ ☆ ☆ ☆ ☆ ☆ ☆ 2 ☆ ☆ ☆ 2 ☆ ☆ ☆ ☆ | 1 |

This flag flew over Fort Sumter where the Civil War began and was used by the Union States between 1859 and 1861. One star was added in 1861 when Kansas joined the Union and another star was added in 1863 when West Virginia joined the Union. The stars for the Confederate states were left on the Union flag because their secession from the Union was considered illegal.

# Harriet Tubman

When Harriet Tubman escaped slavery, she returned to help others escape using a system of safe houses known as the Underground Railroad. She also worked for the Union army during the Civil War. *Unscramble the clues about Harriet's life to find what she said about the Underground Railroad.*

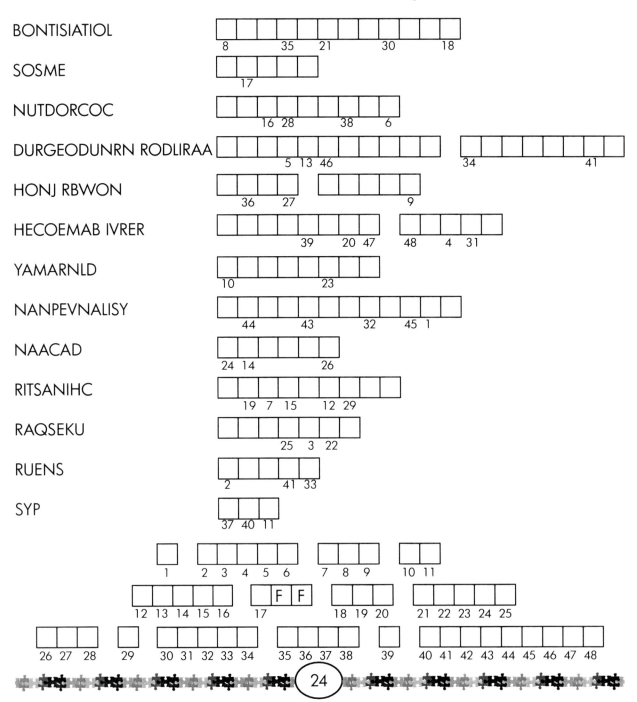

BONTISIATIOL

   8    35   21    30    18

SOSME

  17

NUTDORCOC

  16 28   38   6

DURGEODUNRN RODLIRAA

  5 13 46     34      41

HONJ RBWON

 36  27     9

HECOEMAB IVRER

   39   20 47  48   4  31

YAMARNLD

 10    23

NANPEVNALISY

  44   43   32   45 1

NAACAD

24 14    26

RITSANIHC

  19  7  15   12 29

RAQSEKU

  25  3  22

RUENS

 2    41 33

SYP

37 40 11

1   2 3 4 5 6   7 8 9   10 11

12 13 14 15 16   17 F F   18 19 20   21 22 23 24 25

26 27 28   29   30 31 32 33 34   35 36 37 38   39   40 41 42 43 44 45 46 47 48

# My Ancestor's Journeys

*Whether on the Underground Railroad, a refugee from a war torn area, or on the battlefield, help your ancestor get to safety.*

# Holidays

On October 3rd, 1863, Thanksgiving was made an official national holiday. *Solve the cryptogram to read the first part of the Presidential Proclamation, where Lincoln wrote about being thankful even in the middle of a horrible war.*

| A | B | C | D | E | F | G | H | I | J | K | L | M | N | O | P | Q | R | S | T | U | V | W | X | Y | Z |
|---|---|---|---|---|---|---|---|---|---|---|---|---|---|---|---|---|---|---|---|---|---|---|---|---|---|
|   |   | 23 |   | 14 |   |   |   |   |   |   |   |   |   | 9 |   |   | 12 |   | 19 | 11 |   |   |   |   |   |

```
  T  _  E     _  E  R  T  _  _  T     _  _     R  _  _  _  _  _
 19 22 14     5 14 21 12 19 22 21 19  7 25    15 12 21 26  7 18  6

  T  _  _  _  R  _  _     _  T  _     C  _  _  _  E
 19 10 26 21 12 15 25     7 19 25    23 17 10 25 14

        E  E           _  _  _  _  E  _      _  T  _     T  _  E
 22 21 25  4 14 14 18   24  7 17 17 14 15    26  7 19 22 19 22 14

        E                       _  _        R  _  U  _  T  _  U  _
  4 17 14 25 25  7 18  6 25     10 24       24 12 11  7 19 24 11 17

  _  _  E  _  _  _  _     _  _  _  _  E  _  T  _  U  _  _     _  _  _  E  _
 24  7 14 17 15 25       21 18 15 22 14 21 17 19 22 24 11 17    25  8  7 14 25
```

The rest of the proclamation: To these bounties, which are so constantly enjoyed that we are prone to forget the source from which they come, others have been added, which are of so extraordinary a nature, that they cannot fail to penetrate and soften even the heart which is habitually insensible to the ever watchful providence of Almighty God. In the midst of a civil war of unequaled magnitude and severity, which has sometimes seemed to foreign States to invite and to provoke their aggression, peace has been preserved with all nations, order has been maintained, the laws have been respected and obeyed, and harmony has prevailed everywhere except in the theatre of military conflict; while that theatre has been greatly contracted by the advancing armies and navies of the Union. Needful diversions of wealth and of strength from the fields of peaceful industry to the national defence, have not arrested the plough, the shuttle or the ship; the axe has enlarged the borders of our settlements, and the mines, as well of iron and coal as of the precious metals, have yielded even more abundantly than heretofore. Population has steadily increased, notwithstanding the waste that has been made in the camp, the siege and the battle-field; and the country, rejoicing in the consciousness of augmented strength and vigor, is permitted to expect continuance of

I am thankful for:

```
H  T  M  R  A  W  E  D  U  C  A  T  I  O  N
S  E  H  T  O  L  C  M  F  V  F  F  D  P  H
Y  H  E  A  L  T  H  J  O  R  Q  R  O  S  Y
E  L  G  S  N  U  N  Q  P  H  I  E  O  G  T
Y  T  I  N  U  T  R  O  P  P  O  E  F  N  E
V  U  Q  M  N  S  T  B  R  D  V  D  N  F  F
Z  H  K  B  A  P  H  H  H  O  S  O  T  D  A
O  J  S  D  M  F  V  X  L  E  X  M  B  V  S
```

*Find these blessings in the wordsearch above:*
Family, Friends, Home, Safety, Love, Education, Food,
Clothes, Health, Freedom, Opportunity, Warmth

*Can you write 100 things you are thankful for on another sheet of paper?*

years with large increase of freedom. No human counsel hath devised nor hath any mortal hand worked out these great things. They are the gracious gifts of the Most High God, who, while dealing with us in anger for our sins, hath nevertheless remembered mercy. It has seemed to me fit and proper that they should be solemnly, reverently and gratefully acknowledged as with one heart and one voice by the whole American People. I do therefore invite my fellow citizens in every part of the United States, and also those who are at sea and those who are sojourning in foreign lands, to set apart and observe the last Thursday of November next, as a day of Thanksgiving and Praise to our beneficent Father who dwelleth in the Heavens. And I recommend to them that while offering up the ascriptions justly due to Him for such singular deliverances and blessings, they do also, with humble penitence for our national perverseness and disobedience, commend to His tender care all those who have become widows, orphans, mourners or sufferers in the lamentable civil strife in which we are unavoidably engaged, and fervently implore the interposition of the Almighty Hand to heal the wounds of the nation and to restore it as soon as may be consistent with the Divine purposes to the full enjoyment of peace, harmony, tranquillity and Union.

# Berry Ink

Every soldier anxiously waited for letters from home. They wrote home voraciously trying to solicit more letters from their family and friends. Hundreds of thousands of letters were sent every day during the war. Even through challenges with delivery, most letters were received about two weeks after they were sent.

From:

To:

POSTAGE FIVE CENTS

### Berry Ink

Crush 1/2 cup of berries (strawberries or raspberries) and strain. Add 1/2 teaspoon vinegar and 1/2 teaspoon salt to keep the ink from fading. Cut a feather or hard grass stalk at an angle and practice writing. Blot the ink with a paper towel and allow to dry before folding.

*Confederate soldiers often suffered with shortages of paper, ink and stamps but that didn't keep them from writing to their families. They made ink from berries and used scraps of paper or wrote between the lines of old letters. You can try writing a letter like a Civil War soldier with your own berry ink.*

# A Letter to My Ancestor

*What would you say to your ancestor if you could write to them today?*

Dear _____

Sincerely,

_____

# Oh Yeah?  Prove It.

Documents prove what happened in the past.  What documents have come from your family's life during the Civil War that will prove to someone in the future that they were alive?

*Paste an envelope here.*
*Make copies of documents from your ancestor's life, like*
*letters, census, military, church and probate records and pictures.*
*Store your own copies of these documents in this envelope.*
*Original copies of important items should be kept in a very safe place.*

# Military Messages

The invention of the telegraph just before the Civil War changed the way that commanders could communicate quickly with their officers on the battlefield. The Union army strung 4,000 miles of telegraph wire and sent many messages back and forth to Washington D.C. concerning the battles.

A telegraph machine was used to send Morse Code over the wires. Short dots and long dashes combined together in the code to communicate text to the receiver. Sometimes messages were intercepted from the opposing army and telegraph lines were cut to change what happened on the battlefield.

| A ·− | B −··· | C −·−· | D −·· |
|---|---|---|---|
| E · | F ··−· | G −−· | H ···· |
| I ·· | J ·−−− | K −·− | L ·−·· |
| M −− | N −· | O −−− | P ·−−· |
| Q −−·− | R ·− | S ··· | T − |
| U ··− | V ···− | W ·−− | X −··− |
| Y −·−− | Z −−·· | | |

*Write your ancestor's name here in Morse Code:*

_____

# Music

Music was important in the Civil War.   Bands helped boost morale around the country at home and on  the battlefield.   Here are a few popular songs:

## Union Songs
The lyrics to "When Johnny Comes Marching Home" were written by Patrick Gilmore in 1863.  It is said that he wrote the song for his sister who was praying for the safe return of her fiancé during the Civil War. The melody was previously used as a Civil War drinking song, "Johnny Fill Up the Bowl."

## When Johnny Comes Marching Home

When Johnny comes marching home again
Hurrah! Hurrah!
We'll give him a hearty welcome then
Hurrah! Hurrah!
The men will cheer and the boys will shout
The ladies they will all turn out
And we'll all feel gay
When Johnny comes marching home.
The old church bell will peal with joy
Hurrah! Hurrah!
To welcome home our darling boy,
Hurrah! Hurrah!
The village lads and lassies say
With roses they will strew the way,
And we'll all feel gay
When Johnny comes marching home.

Get ready for the Jubilee,
Hurrah! Hurrah!
We'll give the hero three times three,
Hurrah! Hurrah!
The laurel wreath is ready now
To place upon his loyal brow
And we'll all feel gay
When Johnny comes marching home.
Let love and friendship on that day,
Hurrah, hurrah!
Their choicest pleasures then display,
Hurrah, hurrah!
And let each one perform some part,
To fill with joy the warrior's heart,
And we'll all feel gay
When Johnny comes marching home.

# Confederate Songs

The song "Dixie" originated in minstrel shows of the 1850s, and during the Civil War was adopted as an anthem of the Confederacy. Most sources agree that Daniel Decatur Emmett composed the song, but some claim and argue that others composed it.

## Dixie

I wish I was in the land of cotton,
Old times they are not forgotten;
Look away! Look away! Look away! Dixie Land.
In Dixie Land where I was born in,
Early on one frosty mornin,
Look away! Look away! Look away! Dixie Land.
Old Missus marry "Will-de-weaber,"
Willium was a gay deceaber;
Look away! Look away! Look away! Dixie Land.

But when he put his arm around'er,
He smiled as fierce as a forty-pound'er,
Look away! Look away! Look away! Dixie Land.
Dar's buck-wheat cakes an 'Ingen' batter,
Makes you fat or a little fatter;
Look away! Look away! Look away! Dixie Land.
Den hoe it down an scratch your grabble,
To Dixie land I'm bound to trabble.
Look away! Look away! Look away! Dixie Land

# Military Band Activity

The regiment drummer was very important because the armies used drumbeats to communicate orders to the troops. Army regiments usually marched to the beat of the drum. The weapons used during the civil war generated lots of smoke and it was hard to see during a battle. Likewise, the noise of the guns and fighting made it hard to hear voices. But a regiment could stay together and even receive orders from the drummer. There were signals to march into battle, regroup, and retreat.

## Johnny Clem

Johnny was a boy soldier who joined the Union army when he was only 9 years old. Each side banned boys from fighting, but some boys sneaked into the army by becoming drummers or buglers because they were not officially fighting the enemy. Most people didn't have birth certificates so lying about your age was easy to do. Johnny Clem followed the Michigan 22nd unit and did errands for the soldiers and helped set up camp with them until they let him stay. His drum was smashed by a shell during a battle and he was taken prisoner and returned in exchange for another prisoner. He stayed in the Army and when he grew up he became a general.

*You can make your own Civil War Drum. Start with a paint can or large oatmeal container. Criss cross electrical tape across the top to create the drum surface. Cover the top with fabric and secure with a rubber band. Decorate the sides of the drum with construction paper, rope and drawings. Cover the tops of two pencils with tissue paper and secure with rubber bands. Use the drumsticks to call your regiment to attention.*

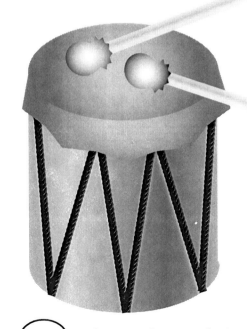

Later in the war, buglers were used to communicate to the troops more than drummers. Regiments heard their bugler so often that they were able to tell their own unit's bugle call from any other bugle sounds. Army bands also played various drums, fifes, bugles, and other horn and drum instruments.

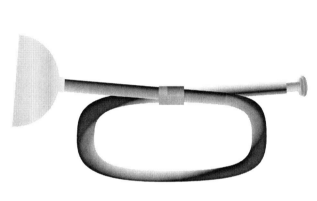

*You can make your own Civil War Bugle. Cut a length of plastic tubing or an old garden hose and use duct tape to create a circle in the hose. Cut the funnel from the top of a 2 liter pop bottle and tape it to one end of the tubing. Use the end of the garden hose for a mouthpiece or purchase an inexpensive trumpet mouthpiece from ebay or a music store. To play the trumpet, put your lips together in an "M" position. Make a buzzing noise into the trumpet and sing the notes of the song.*

*Try some of these bugle calls:*

## Attention

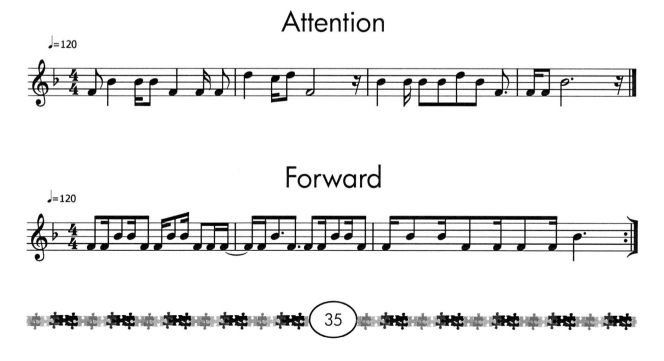

## Forward

*More bugle calls:*

# Fix Bayonets

# Commence Firing

# Cease Firing

# Retreat

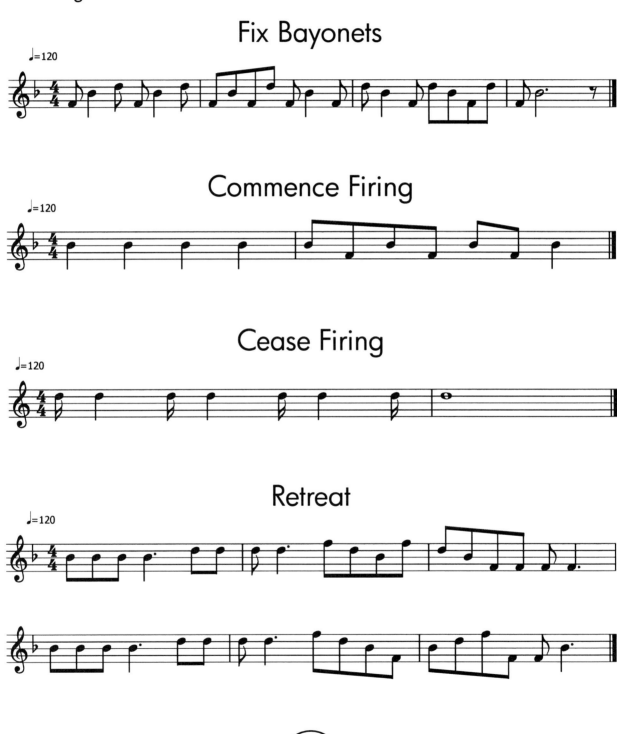

# My Ancestor's Eulogy

*Write a eulogy for your ancestor commemorating the life they lived. Write what you know about their personality, their accomplishments and how they will be remembered in the future.*

✱✱✱✱✱✱✱✱✱✱✱✱✱✱✱✱✱✱✱✱✱✱✱✱✱✱✱✱✱✱✱✱✱

_____

_____

_____

_____

_____

_____

_____

_____

_____

_____

_____

_____

_____

_____

✱✱✱✱✱✱✱✱✱✱✱✱✱✱✱✱✱✱✱✱✱✱✱✱✱✱✱✱✱✱✱✱✱

# War's End

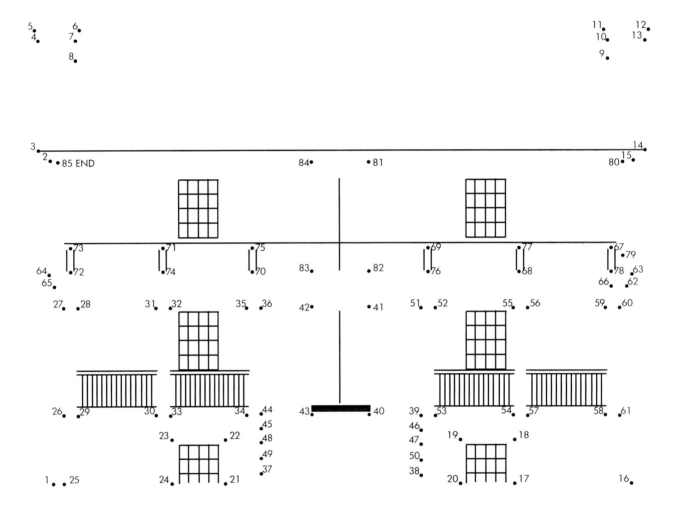

## McLean House at Appomattox, Virginia

On April 9, 1896 the Confederate Army of General Robert E. Lee surrendered to the Union Army of Lt. General Ulysses S. Grant. Lee and Grant met in the parlor of the McLean House in Appomattox, Virginia. The terms of the surrender were generous and none of Lee's men would be imprisoned or tried for treason. They were allowed to take home their horses and given food rations. As Lee left the house Grant's army began to cheer but General Grant ordered them to stop. The way the winning army treated the surrendering army helped heal the people and reconcile the country.

# Paper Dolls

Color and cut out these paper dolls. You can play with them and use them to tell your family members stories about your ancestors.

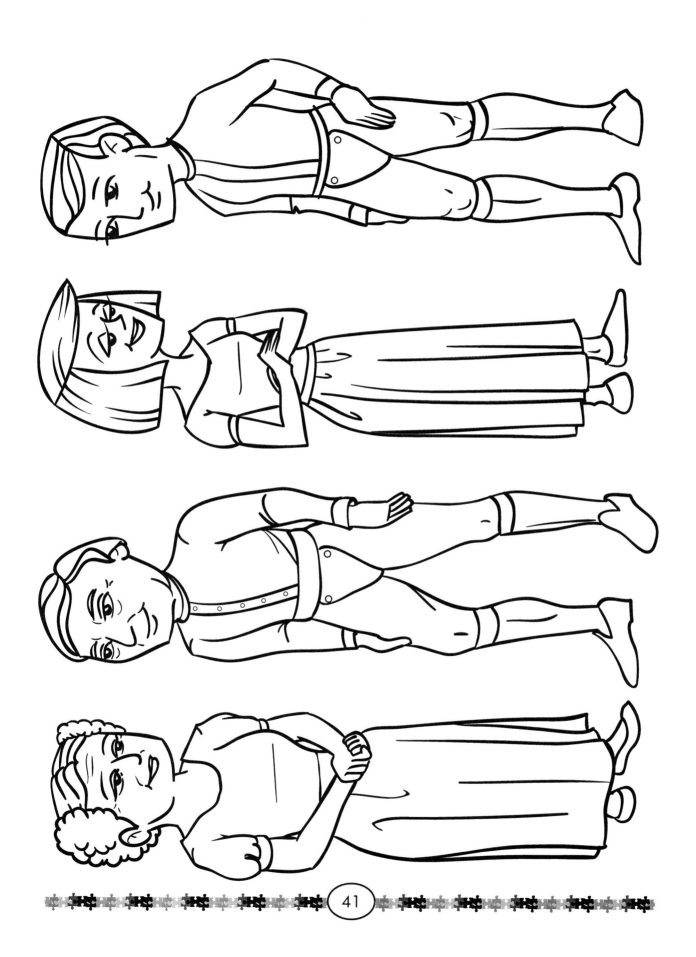

# Paper Doll Clothes

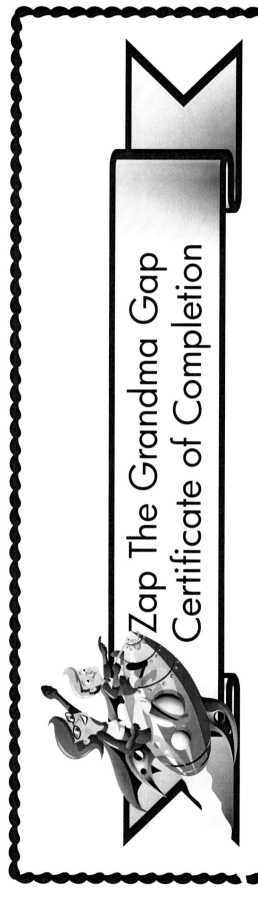

# Zap The Grandma Gap
## Certificate of Completion

_____

has been able to bridge the gap and learn about

_____

their ancestors who lived during the Civil War.

Thanks to _____

for helping complete the activities and research in this workbook.

_____

Date

# Answers

## Abraham Lincoln

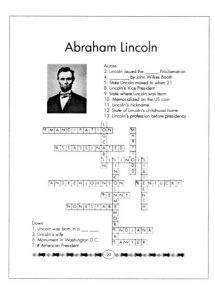

**Across**
2. Lincoln issued the _____ Proclamation
4. _____ by John Wilkes Booth
5. State Lincoln moved to when 21.
8. Lincoln's Vice President
9. State where Lincoln was born
10. Memorialized on the US coin
11. Lincoln's nickname
12. State of Lincoln's childhood home
13. Lincoln's profession before presidency

(crossword solution)
EMANCIPATION
ASSASSINATED
ILLINOIS
ANDREWJOHNSON    KENTUCKY
HONESTABE
MARTYTODD
INDIANA
LAWYER
PENNY

**Down**
1. Lincoln was born in a ___ ___
3. Lincoln's wife
6. Monument in Washington D.C.
7. # American President

## Gettysburg Address

Lincoln's dedication of the cemetery at Gettysburg is considered one of the greatest speeches in U.S. History. Few remember the first speech which lasted for two hours, but Lincoln's short speech is still memorized by many today.
*Rearrange the fallen letters of vertical columns to discover the first part of the speech.*

```
F O U R   S C O R E   A N D   S E V E N
Y E A R S   A G O   O U R   F A T H E R S
B R O U G H T   F O R T H   O N   T H I S
C O N T I N E N T   A   N E W   N A T I O N
C O N C E I V E D   I N   L I B E R T Y
A N D   D E D I C A T E D   T O   T H E
P R O P O S I T I O N   T H A T   A L L   M E N
A R E   C R E A T E D   E Q U A L
```

Now we are engaged in a great civil war, testing whether that nation, or any nation so conceived and so dedicated, can long endure. We are met on a great battlefield of that war. We have come to dedicate a portion of that field, as a final resting place for those who here gave their lives that that nation might live. It is altogether fitting and proper that we should do this.

But, in a larger sense, we can not dedicate, we can not consecrate, we can not hallow this ground. The brave men, living and dead, who struggled here, have consecrated it, far above our poor power to add or detract. The world will little note, nor long remember what we say here, but it can never forget what they did here. It is for us the living, rather, to be dedicated here to the unfinished work which they who fought here have thus far so nobly advanced. It is rather for us to be here dedicated to the great task remaining before us—that from these honored dead we take increased devotion to that cause for which they gave the last full measure of devotion—that we here highly resolve that these dead shall not have died in vain—that this nation, under God, shall have a new birth of freedom—and that government of the people, by the people, for the people, shall not perish from the earth.

## Harriet Tubman

When Harriet Tubman escaped slavery, she returned to help others escape using a system of safe houses known as the Underground Railroad. She also worked for the Union army during the Civil War. *Unscramble the clues about Harriet's life to find what she said about the Underground Railroad.*

BONTISLATIOL — ABOLITIONIST
SOSME — MOSES
NUTDORCOC — CONDUCTOR
DURGEODLUNRN RODLIRAA — UNDERGROUND RAILROAD
RUENS — NURSE
SYP — SPY
YAMARNLD — MARYLAND
NANPEVNALISY — PENNSYLVANIA
NAACAD — CANADA
RITSANIHC — CHRISTIAN
RAQSEKU — QUAKERS
HONJ RBWON — JOHN BROWN
HECOEMAB IVRER — COMBAHEE RIVER

I NEVER RAN MY TRAIN
OFF THE TRACK AND I
NEVER LOST A PASSENGER

## My Ancestor's Journeys

*Whether on the Underground Railroad, a refugee from a war torn area, or on the battlefield, help your ancestor get to safety.*

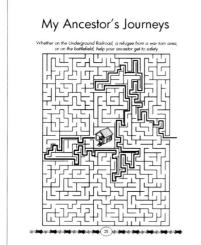

## Holidays

Thanksgiving was made a national holiday on October 3rd, 1863. Solve the cryptogram to read the first part of the Presidential Proclamation, where Lincoln wrote about gratitude for blessings even in the middle of a horrible war.

```
A  B  C  D  E  F  G  H  I  J  K  L  M  N  O  P  Q  R  S  T  U  V  W  X  Y  Z
21    4    23 15       14 24    6                18 10    9       12 25 19 11    26    5
```

THE YEAR THAT IS DRAWING
19 22 14   5 14 21 12   19 22 21 19   7 25   15 12 21 24 7 18 6

TOWARDS ITS CLOSE
19 10 26 21 12 15 25   7 19 25   23 17 10 25 14

HAS BEEN FILLED WITH THE
22 21 25   4 14 14 18   24 7 17 17 14 15   24 7 19 22   19 22 14

BLESSINGS OF FRUITFUL
4 17 14 25 25 7 18 6 25   10 24   24 11 21 7 19 24 17

FIELDS AND HEALTHFUL SKIES
24 7 14 17 15 25   21 18 15   22 14 21 17 19 24 11 17   25 8 7 14 25

To these bounties, which are so constantly enjoyed that we are prone to forget the source from which they come, others have been added, which are of so extraordinary a nature, that they cannot fail to penetrate and soften even the heart which is habitually insensible to the ever watchful providence of Almighty God. In the midst of a civil war of unequaled magnitude and severity, which has sometimes seemed to foreign States to invite and to provoke their aggression, peace has been preserved with all nations, order has been maintained, the laws have been respected and obeyed, and harmony has prevailed everywhere except in the theatre of military conflict; while that theatre has been greatly contracted by the advancing armies and navies of the Union. Needful diversions of wealth and of strength from the fields of peaceful industry to the national defence, have not arrested the plough, the shuttle or the ship; the axe has enlarged the borders of our settlements, and the mines, as well of iron and coal as of the precious metals, have yielded even more abundantly than heretofore. Population has steadily increased, notwithstanding the waste that has been made in the camps, the siege and the battle-field; and the country, rejoicing in the consciousness of augmented strength and vigor, is permitted to expect continuance of years with large increase of freedom.

### I am thankful for:

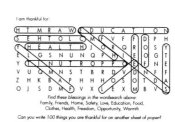

*Find these blessings in the wordsearch above.*
Family, Friends, Home, Safety, Love, Education, Food, Clothes, Health, Freedom, Opportunity, Warmth

*Can you write 100 things you are thankful for on another sheet of paper?*

No human counsel hath devised nor hath any mortal hand worked out these great things. They are the gracious gifts of the Most High God, who, while dealing with us in anger for our sins, hath nevertheless remembered mercy. It has seemed to me fit and proper that they should be solemnly, reverently and gratefully acknowledged as with one heart and one voice by the whole American People. I do therefore invite my fellow citizens in every part of the United States, and also those who are at sea and those who are sojourning in foreign lands, to set apart and observe the last Thursday of November next, as a day of Thanksgiving and Praise to our beneficent Father who dwelleth in the Heavens. And I recommend to them that while offering up the ascriptions justly due to Him for such singular deliverances and blessings, they do also, with humble penitence for our national perverseness and disobedience, commend to His tender care all those who have become widows, orphans, mourners or sufferers in the lamentable civil strife in which we are unavoidably engaged, and fervently implore the interposition of the Almighty Hand to heal the wounds of the nation and to restore it as soon as may be consistent with the Divine purposes to the full enjoyment of peace, harmony, tranquillity and Union.

# Further Resources

**See also the Genealogy Resources on page 8.**
**For more information about life during the Civil War:**

civilwar.org
   Timelines and battlefields, home of the Civil War Trust.
civilwar.si.edu
   Holdings about the Civil War from the Smithsonian Institution.
loc.gov/rr/main/uscw_rec_links/civilwarlinks.html
   Maps, Music and Photos from the Library of Congress.
civilwarhome.com
   A huge collection of links about all aspects of the Civil War.
ehistory.osu.edu/uscw/features/medicine/cwsurgeon
   Information about medical practices during the war.
armoryguards.org/bugle_calls.htm
   Recordings of bugle calls from the Civil War.

**References and Suggested Readings:**

Herbert, Janis.  *The Civil War for Kids.*  Chicago Review Press: Chicago, 1999.
Anderson, Maxine.  *Great Civil War Projects You Can Build Yourself.*
   Nomad Press: White River Junction, Vermont, 2005.
Ratliff, Thomas.  *You Wouldn't Want To Be A Civil War Soldier!*  Scholastic:
   New York, 2013.
Jones, Lynda.  *Mrs. Lincoln's Dressmaker: The Unlikely Friendship of Elizabeth
   Keckley & Mary Todd Lincoln.*  National Geographic: Washington, 2009.
Garrison, Mary.  *Slaves Who Dared: The Stories of Ten African American
   Heroes.*  White Mane Kids: Shippensburg, Pennsylvania, 2002.
Canon, Jill.  *Civil War Heroines.*  Bellerophon Books: Santa Barbara, CA, 2000.

Take a look at **zapthegrandmagap.com** for more ideas and free downloads to explore your family history and make it fun for all ages:

•Get the book *Zap The Grandma Gap: Connect to Your Family By Connecting Them To Their Family History* and its companion *Power Up Workbook* for 100s of easy family history ideas.
•Sign up on the website for the weekly newsletter with one simple idea each week to create stronger bonds in your family.

# More Ancestors

*Use the pages for drawings, information and other things you find out about ancestors who lived during the Civil War.*

CPSIA information can be obtained at www.ICGtesting.com
Printed in the USA
LVOW09s1109040914

402438LV00010B/102/P